D1402236

Enduring
Heritage

Mentoring to Nurture the Next Generation

Romeo P. Stockett, PhD

Order this book online at www.trafford.com
or email orders@trafford.com

Most Trafford titles are also available at major online book retailers.

Printed in the United States of America.

ISBN: 978-1-4669-3832-8 (sc)
ISBN: 978-1-4669-3833-5 (e)

Trafford rev. 07/19/2013

 www.trafford.com

North America & international
toll-free: 1 888 232 4444 (USA & Canada)
fax: 812 355 4082

To Rochelle and my eight mentoring-children and their spouses,
who constantly affirm the importance of caring and
"giving back" by mentoring.

"Life's most persistent and urgent question is, 'What are you doing for others?'"—Martin Luther King, Jr.

CONTENTS

1 Introduction: Enduring Heritage 1

2 The Serious Need For and the Business of Mentoring 13

3 Mentoring Can Take on Many Forms 19

4 Fundamental Characteristics Needed for Mentoring 25

5 Mentoring For a Specific Purpose 29

6 Building a Mentoring Toolkit 35

7 Mini-Mentoring 41

8 Conclusion 45

9 Mentoring Resources 47

CHAPTER ONE
Introduction: Enduring Heritage

Mentoring has always been the method of insuring that heritage, tradition and certain conduct is sustained. There are a number of reasons why the practice of mentoring has become codified in the form of a structured relationship. We have always had persons in our lives that have assisted and guided us through events, circumstances and various difficult periods in our lives. Many of these persons stay with us throughout our lives. Some come and go in an instant, depending on the issues or the times. Others come in and out of our lives at intervals. Consider the relationship of parents to an adult child. The roles change from parent to a mentor-like relationship, because after children have grown and gone out into the world they still look to parents in a mentoring fashion for guidance with their business, personal and professional decisions. There is always the parent-child interest and concern for all matters but the essence of the relationship changes when the parent provides guidance in the mentoring fashion. That is "when a parent and child meet again on a different level." When parents mentor, their guidance is more objective and matter of fact, and less parent to child.

Unfortunately, in recent times, we have seen such a drastic erosion of the family structure and consequently erosion of the roles and responsibilities of family members. It is as if the core, the very nucleus of the concept of the traditional family as been disrupted. This change or disruption has left a void in the guidance and direction of the lives of young adults and children in families. Many parents are perplexed about the methods to provide guidance, discipline and teaching core values to their children because they have not had such direction themselves. In this environment, the dependency on external assistance has become vital to our youths' personal development, their educational advancement, in their interpersonal relationships and other life skills. Consequently, there has evolved the increased need for personal and professional mentoring.

> "Mentoring brings us together—across generation, class, and often race—in a manner that forces us to acknowledge our interdependence, to appreciate, in Martin Luther King, Jr.'s words, that 'we are caught in an inescapable network of mutuality, tied to a single garment of destiny.'

In this way, mentoring enables us to participate in the essential but unfinished drama of reinventing community, while reaffirming that there is an important role for each of us in it."

—Marc Freedman

Personal Mentoring

The need has increased for personal mentoring because our youth and many times their parents have a very difficult time navigating the early complications of personal growth because the parents were not fortunate enough to have proper guidance and/or models themselves. Many parents are without a sound grounding in morality, civility, work ethics, common courtesies, personal and professional core values, and just how to navigate and succeed in the world. And these circumstances have nothing to do with income or education, race or gender, urban or rural. At a time when we are experiencing the erosion of the family nucleus, our youth have to deal with life issues the likes of which we would have never imagined. The negative social pressures and distractions in society, schools, media and adult misconduct are at an all-time high. Youth of today have to deal with serious life issues at a much younger age and with a lot less preparation and adult guidance. Young people today face issues of drugs, sex, violence, motivation, inspiration, social and peer pressures, education and socialization that many of their parents never imaged, and never at such a young age.

These issues are very complicated today, because there are few positive standards of ethics or morality portrayed in mass media, entertainment media and social media. Our youth are inundated with negative images and negative behaviors. Entertainment media is at its all-time worse, portraying loose sexual conduct as situation comedy, where even serious medical, legal and other program series are punctuated with trashy conduct by the leads. Entertainment performers are held in high esteem by the media because reporting on their bad behavior improves their ratings. For these reasons the roles and responsibilities of the personal youth mentor have grown larger and more complicated.

It is because of these reasons that I wanted to share my knowledge, experience, insights and some proven mentoring practices with those in the business of or who are simply interested in assisting others to realize their potential through mentoring. I also hope this book will inspire you to get involved and become a mentor.

Professional Mentoring

The need for mentoring has increased in the professional realm because of the changing roles business and industry play in our lives today. Mostly gone are the opportunities for a career with a particular agency or company where an employee starts at the entry level, stays 30 years, and retires as people did 30 years ago. There was a time when career progression was possible and expected and was actually structured into your relationship with an employer. For instance an employee joined IBM, KODAK, General Motors, any of the large companies or agencies and they could plan to stay with the company for an extended period, and they could plan on some structured career progression even if it was within a specialty and even if the progression was monetary only. People had a retirement track that led to a comfortable income, with health benefits and a pension. This has all changed, now you are not even guaranteed a career in what was traditionally career oriented professions such as the military, post office, the airlines or any other government or private company enterprise.

Therefore the individual becomes his/her own career planner, responsible for establishing processes and strategies to advance his/her career through education, training, transferrable skills development and a charted series of tactics that are a part of a career strategic plan. Under these conditions, the assistance and guidance of a mentor is paramount to an individual's success. So you can see how the evolution of the practice of mentoring and the acceptance of having to be mentored has become a vital function in personal and professional successes.

Mentoring relationships have always been around. The major difference in these times is the necessity for the mentoring guidance. Mentoring has become necessary to augment the former roles of parents, coaches, teachers and professional superiors because the former roles of these persons have changed. Parents spend a lot less time focusing on their children than they do other responsibilities and they have more distractions. Our youth spend more time in front of some sort of electronic screen and with their peers than with their family and love ones. Consequently, they are influenced a great deal by these external entities which can diminish the family influence. The vital life-style roles of *modeling* by parents have changed and in many cases disappeared altogether. On average, parents are younger, more parents are single, many are single by divorce, many are virtually children raising children and too many are grandparents raising their grandchildren. This is not meant to be an indictment of parenthood but merely a statement of fact. The concept of parenting has changed and in my estimation not for the better. What we see today is the increasing need for outside interventions to counter the negative outside influences. These interventions are often in the form of mentoring, which is why I constantly emphasize the *seriousness of the practice of mentoring.*

When I was young, there was a saying about learning life lessons, which was that "you learned them at your father's knee, or some other joint." Do you get it? Knee? Joint? You learned life's lessons where you should from your parents or you learned them where you could, in the "street" or some other "joint" which was a term for a "not so nice" bar or club. But you could rest assured, that you learned them—life lessons that is. But of most importance was *what* you learned. The premise being, that if you learned them at your "father's knee" you learned the right things.

Unfortunately for many of our young people today the father is not there, and even when they are present, their roles and functions have changed, even diminished. Their roles have changed for many reasons but they changed. Many of our current fathers had no fathers. They were raised by parents who did not give their personal development the necessary emphasis. And even today, the father may be in the home but does not have a clue about the issues facing this child.

> "Of all the rocks upon which we build our lives, we are reminded today that family is the most important. And we are called to recognize and honor how critical every father is to that foundation. They are teachers and coaches. They are mentors and role models. They are examples of success and the men who constantly push us toward it. But if we are honest with ourselves, we'll admit that what too many fathers also are is missing—missing from too many lives and too many homes. They have abandoned their responsibilities, acting like boys instead of men. And the foundations of our families are weaker because of it."
>
> —President, *Barack Obama*

There have been many times when I began to establish a mentoring relationship with a student only to find that the parent's request for his/her child to be mentored is because the parent is perplexed about what they can do to assist the child. The parents are young, some were raised without good role models, trying to figure parenting out while trying to parent themselves. Many parents think that children are too old for a one-on-one relationship beyond early childhood, when the reality is the older children benefit the most from and need that type of one-on-one guidance. Many parents believe that television, school, electronic entertainment and electronic communications can fill the void or that there is not a void because the child is so very engaged and not a bother to them. Many parents see television, video games, cell phones and computers as convenient ways to keep the kid "occupied." They fail to see the influence these external entities have, and especially the exposure children get to things that the parents are never aware of.

In this book I am not going to dwell a lot on *why* we need mentoring, because we are where we are, and we recognize the importance of the practice. I want to deal with *how* we can best advance mentoring skills necessary in the age where "mentoring" relationships are necessary and prevalent.

> *"One in four children in the United States is being raised by a single parent—a percentage that has been on the rise and is higher than other developed countries."*

> *"Of the 27 industrialized countries studied by the Organization for Economic Cooperation and Development, the U.S. had 25.8 percent of children being raised by a single parent, compared with an average of 14.9 percent across the other countries.*

> *In the African American community, 72 percent of Black children are raised in a single parent household."—National Children's Count Data Center, 2012*

Mentoring Relationships

Mentoring relationships take on many forms and have varying durations. Many start with young people, and if they are fortunate, many of their first mentors are their family members. Most of the time you don't recognize that parents and relatives fulfill a mentoring role because it is expected that family care about a child's wellbeing and personal success. Helping with the success in school, community life, little league programs, and social activities has been the traditional role of family. Within the family role you don't see these roles as mentoring because labeling it *mentoring* gives the roles structure and parameters, therefore making the relationship more formal than spontaneous. I want my readers to recognize the formal part family and other people play in a child's life so you always recognize these roles when you play them in the lives of others. Many of us mentor without knowing it, which is why I make this distinction. You need to know and recognize mentoring when it happens.

One of the first steps in mentoring is to understand that every human's basic desire and need is to be "heard" and to be "seen." Hearing takes a special effort, because listening to someone's words is not the same as understanding what they are saying about their feelings and thoughts. It is very difficult for many people to frame their thoughts and feeling in words, and therefore it is important for you to build a relationship that is based on trust, understanding and non-judgment in order for you to clear the communications paths from noises that interfere with your opportunity to really hear what your mentee is saying to you. When a person finds someone they feel "hears them", they are very receptive to that person's guidance, and again that is why I constantly emphasize the vital impact a mentor can have on a person's life. Mentors must always be aware that their guidance cannot be given in a cavalier manner. The trust factor in a mentoring relationship is key to the response you get from the mentee and therefore the mentor's guidance must be carefully thought out. As I emphasize throughout this book, mentoring is a very serious relationship.

History of Mentoring

Legend has it that the term **"mentor"** originated in Ancient Greece when Odysseus left to fight in the Trojan War. He entrusted the care of this household to a trusted friend named Mentor. For many years Mentor served as a teacher, advisor and confidant to Telemachus, Odysseus' son. Over time, the word "mentor" came to describe a wise and trusted advisor, friend or teacher.

A more modern-day definition of mentoring is "one who provides information, assistance and guidance to someone of lesser experience and/or knowledge of a particular area. The mentor provides information and guidance based on his or her personal or professional experiences or learnings."

This modern-day definition has evolved from the industrial revolution, the growth of government agencies, the vast growth of the small business industries, and educational institutions. So over the past

70 years, mentors were primarily those who assisted with education and/or professional development. As it has evolved, professional mentoring was a kind of professional, sterile relationship, "strictly business." There were some things that the mentee needed to learn and understand and the role of the mentor was to guide them through their education, experiences and practice. Once the mentee was acclimated, the relationship with that mentor ended.

Today, however, mentoring relationships have become much more complicated because the personal and professional environment has become more complex.

CHAPTER TWO
The Serious Need For and the Business of Mentoring

The cry for someone to "show me the way" either up or out of a situation has become epidemic—up from where I find myself or out of the mess in which I find myself. The call is for more than a professional or someone more experienced to look at what I am attempting to do, but more of an urgent cry for personal assistance. For example, help me see where I am, help me plan for a change, help me implement my plan and be there for me as I navigate the waters ahead. This cry is loud and clear from so many of our young men and women, and it is echoed for them by their parents, guardians, spouses and other family members. I am constantly overwhelmed with the constant unsolicited requests for some form of mentoring from a parent for a young person who has or is in danger of "losing their way." I was raised in a very nurturing and cultivating community. All the adults wanted us to be better, even the "not so good people." In those days the neighborhood was made up of people of all types and income levels, the blue collars, the professionals and the scholars were all within walking distance of each other.

Long before the practice of mentoring was codified, elders taught young people life-skills. They taught them the basic skills for survival; they taught them of their culture their roles in that culture and their responsibilities to their family, community and themselves. The elders modeled the behaviors they desired for the youth and admonished them on the unacceptable behaviors. They not only gave them lessons but they gave them tools and directions for success. And of most importance, the elders taught the young people values—the cultural, personal and community values. These values included attitudes toward acquiring knowledge, being charitable, respect, honesty and hard work. As for my personal experience, it was rich in mentoring relationships. My elders taught us young people the good, the bad and the ugly. There was no "sugar coating." My elders taught us the "real deal". They were always clear when telling us what life would be like without an education. They taught us and showed us the importance of personal strength when faced with adversity, and the real meaning of honesty and the consequences of dishonesty. As far back as I can remember, the adults in my life may not have always displayed the best behaviors, but I always knew they wanted the best for me. My memories of some of the "not so good people" was that they wanted better for me too because they would always say "don't grow up to be like me" and they really meant it.

Since I left home at 17 and joined the Air Force, I look back on my early years as a time when I was always embraced and affirmed. I always felt cared for and was always reminded of my value. It was at that early age of adulthood, when I began to meet other young people from all parts of the country who did not have benefit of a nurturing early life and who were struggling to figure things out, that I realized how fortunate I was. It was then that I made a commitment that I would always work to "be there" for others. Now more than ever we need to "be there" for each other and especially for our youth. That was over 50 years ago, and that is how I have lived my life, always willing to share my knowledge, experience, time, attention, and ear, and talk with those who desire the support.

As human beings there is always something you can share with another individual and especially our youth, even if you can just provide the opportunity for them to talk with someone who will listen without judging them.

"Statistics and Research

Research confirms what we knew anecdotally or intuitively before—that mentoring works. A Research Brief published by Child Trends and titled "Mentoring: A Promising Strategy for Youth

Development" found that youth who participate in mentoring relationships experience a number of positive benefits.

- *In terms of educational achievement, mentored youth have better attendance; a better chance of going on to higher education; and better attitudes toward school.*
- *In terms of health and safety, mentoring appears to help prevent substance abuse and reduce some negative youth behaviors.*
- *On the social and emotional development front, taking part in mentoring promotes positive social attitudes and relationships. Mentored youth tend to trust their parents more and communicate better with them."*

Building a Mentoring Relationship

It is important for you to meet the mentee "where they are" and that means where they are mentally, emotionally, physically, level of education and beliefs. It is important that you build the relationship based on respect and understanding versus subordinate and superior.

It is also important to understand that a mentoring relationship must have parameters without appearing to be so structured as to interrupt communications. If the mentee is a child, the role of the mentor should not be confused with nor diminish the roles of parents, teachers, or other responsible adults in a child's life.

In particular, over the past 50 years the Black Community has suffered from the very successes that we struggled so hard to achieve. We have made great strides in professional growth, economic advances, political office, lifestyles and social status. All of this progress was on the shoulders of "mentors." They took the form of parents, friends, educators, bystanders, and for many, on the shoulders of "angels." However, all this progress came at a great expense to our families, schools, sense of community (we may still live together but the spirit of community has been lost), personal relationships and the relationship with our youth. That is one of the reasons that mentoring has taken on a more complex and impactful nature in the Black Community. Professional mentoring has grown from the progress made in education and business career successes and the growth of small businesses in our community. Personal coaching and mentoring has grown with the difficulties that the societal changes have caused in our families, marriages, youth rebellion and the fragmentation of our communities.

More than ever, today we must be there for each other, and especially our youth. Today, the childhoods of youth are so very contracted because they are exposed to the issues of the world far in advance of their age and so adult intervention is needed with a new sense of urgency.

"Data clearly show many youths have a desperate need for positive role models. The most compelling data describe changes to the American family structure: the number of single-parent homes has radically increased, as have two-parent working families. More preventive care is needed, as are support networks

to fill the void left by busy or absent parents. Other statistics are equally troubling: each day in the United States, 3,600 students drop out of high school, and 2,700 unwed teenage girls get pregnant (Petersmeyer 1989)."

CHAPTER THREE
Mentoring Can Take on Many Forms

Mentoring takes on many time-limited forms but they all fit certain assumptions when you are in a mentoring relationship such as, mentoring someone through a period of mourning or during a job search period.

I mentor in many forms and fashions. Some of my mentees and I have a formal relationship, with structured times and places to do planned events. All the activities are developed around the purpose of the mentoring relationship. It might be for the advancement of his education or preparing her for a professional career. Regardless, it always involves personal growth and development. I am committed to young people having a successful and enjoyable youth while working on those things that make them a "quality" person of the highest character.

Other of my mentoring relationships are spontaneous, and with people I encounter but do not know. I never pass up the opportunity to acknowledge good and bad behavior, without being aggressive and while respecting everyone as individuals. We all have needed a little reminder from time to time and wish that someone was there who cared enough to remind us. The point that I always emphasize is that I intervene because I care about them even though I don't "know" them, they are important to me, to us, to this world. Other times I just pass them one of my "thought" cards that simply says:

> "You are of great value to yourself, to your family, to us as a community, and especially to this world. Ask yourself, 'Are you treasuring yourself?' You have potential beyond your wildest imagination so never let this world define you."

In the formal mentoring relationship, I always establish a sense of purpose. What are we expecting from the relationship? Try to keep clear each of our expectations. The expectations change as the relationship grows, and so there are times when you have to re-negotiate the terms of the relationship. Whenever possible I encourage my mentees to be mentors to someone else because the best way to reinforce something you have learned is to teach it to someone else. As I said, there is benefit in the relationship for both the mentor and mentee. It gives youths and adults a sense of responsibility and commitment.

The terms of a mentoring relationship are defined by the purpose of the relationship. For example, a youth mentoring relationship might be limited to assisting the youth with personal development, academic pursuits, and/or family interpersonal issues. The relationship with an adult might be based on career transition, professional development, or as in some of my many mentoring relationships, it is on a general basis and my mentee consults with me on many different issues regarding their professional or personal life at various points in time.

Some mentoring relationships are very structured and others are less structured.

The Structured Mentoring Relationship

I recommend for the parties involved in a structured mentoring relationships to do the following:

a. Write an agreement outlining the terms, objectives and some definition of completion.
b. Establish time lines
c. Establish each party's roles, responsibilities and expectations, and remember that sustaining the relationship should be the responsibility of the mentee and the mentor.
d. Clarify any boundaries in order to guard against scope creep and so that each party has a clear and consistent understanding. For example, with a given student, you

want to specify that the mentoring relationship is limited to academic pursuits. Note: it is impossible to have a mentoring relationship with a student without getting personally involved and that's Ok, as long as you recognize the extent and you ensure that it does not complicate the youth's relationship with his/her parents, guardians, and others. You also want to guard against a co-dependency relationship developing. Co-dependency can be debilitating to the mentee and hampers progress because neither partner wants to move on.

e. Have some criteria for assessing and evaluating progress so you know when there is a need for changing directions, and for determining when the mentoring relationship should be terminated.

The Unstructured Mentoring Relationship

There will be circumstances where your mentoring engagement will be less structured, such as when the mentee is at university, the relationship is long distance, when each of you decides to have it less structured or when the mentoring is limited to providing support over a specific personal or career challenge. I have had mentees who were serving in the military so we selected periods when we would consult, such as, each month of basic training, upon completion of basic when they were on their way to technical or advanced training, and then when they received their first permanent assignment. After that, we talk periodically for what we call "how goes it" just to stay in touch. During these conversations, sometimes the mentee is not really in need of advice or direction but rather wants an opportunity for the mentor to simply be a sounding board for them as s/he navigates the changes and issues in their life.

In the informal approach there might be a series of meetings in the beginning with the mentee to clarify the objectives, sort out possible approaches to the desired outcomes and provide them with some direction, tools and resources that will assist them in reaching their goals.

This type of mentoring is conducive to circumstances when a periodic contact is sufficient rather than an on-going consistent contact. The mentor-mentee meeting times can be agreed upon based on milestones, when selected objectives are met, on a calendar basis or when one or the other persons needs a consultation or update. However, this casual schedule should be set within specific time parameters such as over the next 6 months, or during the next semester, the next job performance period, etc.

The periodic follow-up sessions may be in person, electronically or by phone. However, even though the format is casual there should be accurate records kept of the goals, objectives and periodic meeting outcomes. In the casual or informal approach to mentoring it is very important that you set clear start and completion times or events. For example, until the mentee is accepted into medical school, graduates from high school, gets the job or position the mentee is working toward, or when each party agrees on a timeline. The timeline could be set on a calendar year, and at the end of the period the mentor and mentee will assess the progress and either establish a new period, set new goals and objectives or simply agree to terminate.

Just know that termination does not necessarily mean the termination of the entire relationship. You may decide to reestablish the mentoring relationship at some point in the future, such as after the mentee has completed his/her professional education and is now entering the workforce. The relationship might be re-established when the mentee is in need of professional development to achieve a higher level in their career progression. As for my military mentees, we might re-establish the relationship when they transition back into the civilian workforce or return to school with their GI Bill benefits.

CHAPTER FOUR

Fundamental Characteristics Needed for Mentoring

The first and most important personal characteristic for a mentor is to be **non-judgmental** and to have **sincerity.** It is important that you meet the mentee where they are and make no judgment about where you think they should be. You need to accept people where they are and be able to commit to building a relationship from there. You must give them **respect** and always preserve their **dignity.** And by doing so, you teach them how to be respectful and how to display dignity.

Be sure that you are sincere in your interest and concern for them as a person, and be committed to building a relationship that will assist them in their particular goals. Those goals might be as simple as learning to read better, enhancing their relationship with siblings and friends, or as complex as preparing them for acceptance to the school of engineering. The complexity of the goals does not matter, it is the commitment to the relationship and the **honest communications** that will help you succeed in the goals.

Another characteristic fundamental to commitment is **availability.** Can you actually be available for them? And today with youths' busy schedules the question is also, whether you can meet them where they are in their lives and can you go to school events, go to games, field trips, and other activities they may have and of which they may want you to be a part. That level of involvement might not always be needed, but if it is, can you be available?

And with all those characteristics in play, you then must be able to **listen** and be **tolerant** of what you hear. Do not pass judgment on the messenger of the message. Young people have a lot of serious concerns, and some not so serious but are serious to them. But we need only remember the traumas that we experienced at a young age and the difficulty they caused us in later life, or the benefit of having someone mentor us to better outcomes. Being tolerant and non-judgmental does not mean that you approve of and accept everything the mentee does. Rather, it simply means that you do not judge the mentee's "worthiness" or "value" as a person based on these things. All people are worthy and deserving of your attention and care.

And lastly, and perhaps the most important, is **preparation.** Remember," **action speaks louder than words,"** which means you need to model the behavior you want your mentee to emulate. Be prepared to meet with them, be true to your promises—if you are supposed to do something be sure it's done. Demonstrate a "no excuse" system, teach them what it means to be prepared, and remember, preparation is a testament to your commitment to whatever you are doing. They need to know that you are constantly committed.

It is important for you to be able to listen to their concerns without ever conveying judgments to them about their parents, teachers, siblings, and other adults in their lives. Know that what they are giving you is their perspective of events in their life and so it is important to remember you are there for them, to assist them with their development, assist them with managing their environment and circumstances in life, not to pass judgments on anyone.

CHAPTER FIVE
Mentoring For a Specific Purpose

I had a mentor with a purpose long before mentoring became popular. It was 1945 and The War had ended, the big War, WWII, and there were many returning veterans in our neighborhood. We were so very proud of them and they wore their uniforms for almost a year after they got out of the military, many because they had no other clothes and others because of the personal and national pride.

My sister and I were struggling to recover from diseases that killed young people in those days. She had polio which is an infectious, virus-caused disease with inflammation of the gray matter of the spinal cord, often resulting in physical disablement. I had rheumatic fever, an inflammatory reaction of the heart, usually involving the valves as a consequence of streptococcal infection. At any rate, after a long period in Children's Hospital I came home very weak and with a bleak future because recovery in my case was not expected. Actually my parents were told that I would not live pass 10 years of age.

My sister had been in Children's Hospital with me and was released with steal braces on her legs (braces like "Forest Gump" and President FD Roosevelt). Her prognosis was not good, and we thought she would never walk again without aids.

When we were released from the hospital, we were home alone through the day. Both of our parents worked, so they would get us up, feed us breakfast, notify the neighbors on both sides of our house that they were leaving for work and we would take care of each other all day, knowing that if we had any problems that we could call on either of the neighbors. We only called on neighbors when and if a storm came up and we were scared to stay in the house alone, or if they were having something we liked for lunch and sometimes dinner.

And so our day consisted of breakfast, cleaning up, we had chores everyday, and school work. We lived right across the street from Lenox Elementary school and Ms. Garner was our teacher. Even though my sister was two years older and higher in grade, Ms. Garner taught both of us. She would deliver our assignments on Fridays. We worked on them over the weekend and the following week. Sometimes she would come over and bring us lunch from the cafeteria, and we would act very appreciative but it was the worst tasting stuff. When she left we would give it to Ricky, our little raggedy dog.

A few houses down a new neighbor moved in. He was single, a returning veteran, going to Howard University on the GI Bill and driving a cab at night. He was a very smart and proud young man of about 27. He had just gotten a new Capital cab, I think it was a new Plymouth, black and shinny. And he kept it that way, washing and wiping it down every day.

My sister and I would spend our mornings and afternoons on the front porch doing our studies, playing around and watching our classmates at recess across the street. I was very weak and was not ever supposed to exert myself and my sister had those braces on her legs. And the braces were utility only, nothing pretty, very heavy, and very stiff, which made walking very laborious. So there we would be on the porch all day.

One day I saw Mr. Warner, the new neighbor and veteran, carrying boxes and things into his house. Something was visible and looked like guns, helmets, and other war relics. These were things he had shipped from overseas and were just arriving here. In those days it took weeks, sometimes months for shipments from overseas. I could not handle not knowing what all that interesting stuff was. So I asked, and that was the beginning of our relationship.

He began to show me all sorts of military paraphernalia he had collected during the European campaigns in which he fought, things from France, Germany, Italy, North Africa and Russia. Each week it was a different item and a long story. And every night I would look up the places he talked about in our encyclopedias so I would be ready for the next story about the next place.

After about a week of me visiting with him and him telling me all these fascinating stories, one day he asked me "Why are you always home and sitting around on the porch doing nothing?" "You should be out racing and running like the other kids."

I was reluctant to attempt to tell him what my problem was because I thought he might not like to talk to me anymore. But I attempted anyway. I said "I have rheumatic fever" and he said, kiddingly, "Is that why they named you Romeo?" He did not have a clue what I was talking about and thought I said "romantic fever." We got a good laugh out of it and that became our personal joke. He would always say, all you have to do is change your name and you will get better.

But one day I realized that he had done his homework and had researched rheumatic fever, polio and FDR. When we were talking about it one day he said, you just have a "weak heart" right? And I said yes. He said to me "you know the heart is a muscle and like any muscle you have to work it in order for it to get stronger." And so in typical GI language, I learned a lot of that from him, he said "you need to get off your ass, race and run and strengthen your heart muscle."

I told him if I did that it would kill me. He said "what the hell, you gonna die anyway, isn't that what you told me?" "So would you rather die sitting on the porch and let all your friends have all the fun?" He asked me, do you trust me? Remember I was about 6 or 7 years old and yes, I trusted him.

He was equally as concerned about my sister and he began assisting her with walking with her braces but was not as involved because polio at that time was thought to be a permanent disability. But for me, he would take me to a park about a block away in the morning and started me climbing the monkey poll, pushing me in the swing so high I thought my nose would bleed. Eventually he started me running, a little at first and then just all out. Most important was the conversations he had with me, all about what a "man" was suppose to be. Macho stuff like strong, brave, never cry, never weak, tough, combative, aggressive, he even taught me how to "stare a man down." That stuff was important to him and it became important to me. And he related all this stuff to my condition. He would say "strengthen your mind, will strengthen your body, will strengthen that 'piece of a heart you got'."

After working-out and running around, he would make me go over to a stone water fountain and had me wash my face so my parents did not know what I had been doing. We did not do changes of clothes in those days.

After about three or four months of this, the school was having a Field Day marking the end of school. They were having all kinds of field events like races, high jump, tug-of-war, and so forth. I begged my parents to take me and once there they were surprised to know that I was one of the participants. Ms. Garner had allowed me to sign up to run, Sgt. Warner had conditioned me and I had a great day. I did not win a single event but I ran that day and have not stopped running since.

That was an incident of **"mentoring for a specific purpose,"** which helped me through a very difficult time. Now, I don't share this story to encourage you to give "medical advice" as a mentor, in fact, I would warn against it. This is just a true example of a positive mentoring relationship that I experienced in my life and one for which I remain grateful.

Sgt. Warner was from Mississippi and had planned to make his life in D.C. but one of his parents became ill and he left to take care of them. I never saw him again but his impact on my life was indelible. He not only strengthened my heart physically, he strengthened my belief in myself, he taught me to trust, he gave me models to model after, some good some not so good, but he also showed me the importance of discerning. Because of my success and Sgt. Warner's efforts, my sister was so encouraged that her rehabilitation was like a miracle and she eventually was able to shed her braces and by the time she was in 6th grade she was on the dance team, played volley ball and never looked back.

CHAPTER SIX
Building a Mentoring Toolkit

Mentees Need More Than Talk, They Also Need Modeling and "Tools"

Mentoring is the exercise of sharing information and experience and providing guidance for someone less knowledgeable or experienced. That aspect of mentoring is the very basis of the practice. However, mentoring today has become more complex because issues for youth and professionals have become more complex. And so, unlike in the past when you might have been effective by simply providing information and encouragement for a youth seeking higher education, to stay in school, for finding a job, today they require more. They need to know what it looks like and what is involved in seeking a higher education. They need to know what planning looks like, in other words modeling the behavior or practice you expect them to perform. They need to know what researching for job opportunities looks like and the detailed steps. As you know, when you tell someone they need to "take more initiative" for instance, to them, what does that mean and how does that look and most important what actual activities lead to "taking more initiative?"

Mentors need to prepare and constantly increase their mentoring "toolkit." They need to have a file of practices, procedures, strategies, task lists, checklists, and documented examples of how to get things done for themselves as well as for their mentee. For example, what does it take to "never be late?" It is a great deal more than just showing up at an appointed time. It means planning for the day's events, knowing the proper attire and planning for what you will wear, ensuring your transportation, other scheduled events, materials needed for the event, pre-reading of any instructions or materials to be discussed, calling for confirmation of appointment time and date, arriving 20 minutes prior to the scheduled time in order to be prepared for any unexpected changes or issues, and also letting someone know you have arrived and are waiting.

Another example of when and how tools and guidance are crucial is in the area of seeking scholarship opportunities or actually applying for a scholarship program. You might have had an occasion in the past when you have given a student or their parents information of a scholarship, then see them some time later and ask about how the application went or to find out they never completed, and in some cases never started the application process. The reality is as a mentor you have failed to recognize the complexities involved and the limited understanding of students and many parents of how to prepare an effective application. First and foremost is advocacy. Students need an advocate who will assist them in navigating the research and application process. They need assistance in comprehending the scholarship criteria and how to formulate the presentation of their education and experience to qualify. They need assistance in determining what support documents they need to submit and how to secure these documents, such as transcripts, letters of reference, course and training experiences and their personal statement.

All these things are important because in addition to applying, their application must be properly prepared and competitive. The application should be a representation of the student's quality of work, and must be submitted before the deadline.

So I hope you see the importance of "mentoring tools" because they provide the "how to" steps for your mentee to complete an assignment. They guarantee success and that's what we all are working towards. But most important they enhance the relationship because the tools reduce the frustration for both parties that are result of you as the mentor telling the mentee to do something and them doing the very best they can with their limited understanding of how to get it done and consequently being frustrated and you disappointed.

You do not have to have tools developed all at once prior to mentoring. Simply develop or collect them over time. Also, you can record them in whatever format works best for you and is useful and understandable by your mentee. So start now to accumulate your mentoring arsenal of "tools" they will greatly increase successful outcomes.

"A recent highly-comprehensive study conducted by Communities In Schools and the National Dropout Prevention Center at Clemson University (Dropout Risk Factors) identified a variety of predictive risk factors for dropping out. The report states that while there is no single risk factor that causes dropping out, each additional risk factor an individual faces increases the likelihood of dropping out. Some of the key alterable risk factors the study cites are:

- *Teen parenthood*
- *Substance abuse*
- *Criminal behaviors*
- *Lack of self-esteem*
- *Poor school performance/Grade retention*
- *Absenteeism*
- *Discipline problems at school*
- *Low educational expectations/Lack of plans for education beyond high school; and*
- *Lack of interaction with extracurricular activities.*

Mentoring and Academic Achievement

- *High school graduation is an economic imperative in today's global economy driven by knowledge and* innovation. *Mentoring is a positive youth development strategy that supports the goal of reducing the dropout rate by 50 percent over the next five years. Research has shown that mentoring has significant positive effects on two early indicators of high school drop-outs: high levels of absenteeism (Kennelly & Monrad, 2007) and recurring behavior problems (Thurlow, Sinclair & Johnson, 2002). A landmark Public/Private Ventures evaluation of Big Brothers Big Sisters programs showed that students who meet regularly with their mentors are 52 percent less likely than their peers to skip a day of school. An analysis of mentoring program evaluations conducted by Jekielek, Moore and Hair found that youth in mentoring relationships present better attitudes and behaviors at school and are more likely to attend college than their counterparts.*

- *Dropping out of school is not a singular event but rather the culmination of a long process of disengagement. It is critical that intervention efforts aimed at students with a disproportionate number of risk indicators for dropping out of high school reach students young enough. Children between 9 and 15 are commonly at important turning points in their lives. It is during this time that they may permanently turn off from serious engagement in school life and turn to a variety of risky behaviors that can limit their chances of reaching productive adulthood. Encouragingly, this is also the age bracket during which preventative intervention is most successful and youth are most capable of envisioning a positive future and plotting*

<u>the steps they need to take to reach their goals</u>. They are at the right stage of development to best absorb and benefit from the skills of a strong mentor (Rhodes and Lowe, 2008)."

CHAPTER SEVEN
Mini-Mentoring

Taking the Opportunity to Talk On a Chance Encounter

The mentoring needs of our youths, young parents, and professionals, and the unavailability and unwillingness of so many to mentor has created a chasm between the needs and the delivery. I realize so many times that we encounter those who are in need of a word of encouragement, kindness, non-judging concern, or just a few words to get them back on the right track.

I have established a practice for these occasions and I call it "mini-mentoring" or "drive-by" mentoring sessions. You know what I mean because we have all had people who were total strangers that passed through our lives and for a brief moment impart words of insight out of mere interest and concern for who we are. No vested interest, just a caring thought and exchange. I meet so many people to whom I want to reach out, and because of time and circumstances I will only have that one encounter, so I have developed a strategy and a script for these encounters.

First let me say, you might think this practice very risky or ineffective because they are quick and fleeting events and with a total stranger. Not so at all. First of all the biggest response I have received is gratitude because as a total stranger I have shown an interest in them, I have met them where they are, and I have not made any judgment about them. Also, they have a high regard for someone showing an interest in them who has no motive or vested interest. In most cases you will never realize the impact you have had, except to reflect on the times when it happened to you or someone you know.

When you encounter a youth that is clearly "acting out" some bad or unacceptable behavior and if you are conformable with the idea that they are not committing a crime or engaging in dangerous conduct, intercede.

This is how it works. I have a standard script when approaching a young person, which I vary slightly according to their profile and the circumstances. I always introduce myself, indicate why I wanted to talk with them and give them a time frame, such as, "Can we talk for 5 minutes?" They are a little taken aback initially but when they see my sincerity, that is over almost immediately. I ask about them and what they are doing (in school? Working?, etc.), responding and building on whatever they say. I express my concern and interest in their welfare and life goals and then use my list of sources for referrals, I mention things they can read, persons and sites they can visit, and give them some personal insights. I end with encouraging them to stay safe, drug-free and strong and tell them how they are so very important to their family, community and the world.

I encourage you to do some Mini sessions. You may not feel comfortable or effective in the beginning but trust me and yourself, as you get better, you will get better responses, and pretty soon you will realize the value these sessions are to others. We have heard the African principle of "It Takes a Village" to raise a child. This is one of the ways to be part of that village.

DO NOT do this if you are not sincerely concerned and interested in the welfare of a stranger, because insincerity will bleed through and you both will be uncomfortable because it will be perceived as criticism. You must address all your pre-judging, forget who they are, how they look, smell or wear their clothes. Look into their eyes and see yourself there because they are you and me. Work on your fear of rejection and the fear and prejudice we live with about our own youth and go for it!

CHAPTER EIGHT
Conclusion

I sincerely hope you now understand the importance and the increasing need for mentoring in our Community. Likewise, I hope you feel the pull and responsibility for **YOU** to get involved and be a mentor as often and to as many people of all ages and various reasons as possible.

We come from a long and culturally rich "**heritage**" that has been passed along to us from generations past. If we are to help to ensure that this generation and those to follow are equipped to carry on and uplift this sacred heritage so that it can "**endure**", we must each do our part to pass this great heritage forward. Our youth need you, we need each other, and the "village" needs us all.

It is for this purpose that I encourage you to be a serious mentor and ask you to play your part in passing along and ensuring that we have an

"ENDURING HERITAGE"

MENTORING RESOURCES

WHAT ARE SOME EXAMPLES OF MENTORING PROGRAMS? Traditional programs such as Big Brothers/Big Sisters have been joined by school-based programs, independent living skills programs, court-mandated programs, and recreational "buddy" programs. Religious, social, fraternal, civic, professional associations and non-profit youth and family development organizations are engaged in mentoring. Increasingly, older youth are encouraged to volunteer as part of their educational requirements.

- **100 Black Men Of America, Inc,** established in 1963, is a men's civic and service organization whose goal is to educate and empower <u>African American</u> children and teens. The organization's mission statement is "to improve the quality of life within our communities and enhance educational and economic opportunities for all African Americans." The organization's mottos "real men giving real time" and "what they see is what they'll be" describe the organization's goals of providing positive role models and leaders to guide the next generation of African Americans and other youth. It is a nonprofit organization whose members are predominantly <u>African American</u> professionals, businessmen, civic leaders and administrators, educators, as well as people from other walks of life.

- **Big Brothers/Big Sisters of America** provides quality volunteer and professional services to help children and youth become responsible men and women. It is a national, youth-serving organization based on the concept of a one-to-one relationship between an adult volunteer and an at-risk child, usually from a one-parent family. Made up of more than 495 agencies located across the country, Big Brothers/Big Sisters of America provides children and youth with adult role models and mentors who help enrich the children's lives, as well as their own, through weekly interaction. Volunteers go through a screening process before acceptance. Professional case workers provide assistance, support, and on-going supervision of all matches.

- **Help One Student To Succeed** is a nationwide, structured mentoring program in language arts that combines community mentors, a computerized database, and a management system to improve student achievement. The program can be purchased and administered by school districts for use in grades K-12. It is now being utilized in over 500 schools in the country and has won numerous awards. Almost 40,000 students are involved.

- **The National One-to-One Mentoring Partnership**, formed in 1989 between business and the volunteer sector, is a mentoring initiative involving dual strategies. It brings together leaders of diverse sectors and encourages them to mobilize people within their networks to recruit mentors, support existing mentoring programs, and begin new mentoring initiatives. Local Leadership Councils then engage leaders, community by community, with support from the local United Way, in a coordinated effort to develop local strategies to increase and support mentoring initiatives.

ABOUT THE AUTHOR

 Dr. Romeo P. Stockett, Jr. has been a mentor to hundreds of men, women, students, youths, and people of all ages, backgrounds and life circumstances. Everyone who knows him knows of his willingness to provide assistance and guidance to persons in difficult situations or those who are just perplexed about future plans whether personal or professional.

Dr. Romeo Stockett is a retired United States Air Force Officer, University Associate Professor, and a Public Health Care Professional and lives in Stone Mountain, Georgia. Originally from Washington DC, Dr. Stockett spent 30 years in the Air Force before retiring to reside in Georgia. Throughout his military and civilian professional years, Dr. Stockett has directed large military and civilian organizations, held positions in training and education and is currently very active in numerous mentoring practices. He has established mentoring programs in many and varied organizational environments, including education, government, private and non-profit community service agencies. He has consulted with refugee and immigrant communities to assist in developing culturally sensitive mentoring programs in youth development and parent-peer mentoring.

Dr. Stockett was named Mentor of the Year 2009 by the 100 Black Men of America, Inc., a prominent mentoring and youth development organization, in which he holds the position of Chairman of The Youth Leadership Academy, Vice Chairman of the National Health and Wellness Committee and member of the Board of Directors, DeKalb County Chapter. Dr. Stockett was selected by the students of Morehouse School of Medicine, Masters in Public Health program as Outstanding Professor of the Year 2008. In 2012 he received a US Congressional Citation for his outstanding work in advancing Prostate Cancer awareness and education.

Dr. Stockett has devoted his professional and personal life to the practice of sharing his experience and knowledge with others to enhance their personal and professional growth. He and his wife/Business Partner, Rochelle, have 8 children between them. The entire family is committed to giving back through mentoring.